T0362666

GET AHEAD IN GRAMMAR

A practical guide for students

Second edition
Anne Quill
Anne Townsend

Get Ahead in Grammar: A Practical Guide for Students
2nd Edition
Anne Quill
Anne Townsend

Associate publishing editor: Sam Bonwick
Project editor: Mandy Herbet
Editor: Mandy Herbet
Proofreader: Nadine Anderson-Conklin
Cover design: Aisling Gallagher
Text design: Jennai Lee Fai
Production controllers: Julie McArthur and Emma Roberts
Typeset by: Q2A Media

Any URLs contained in this publication were checked for currency during the production process. Note, however, that the publisher cannot vouch for the ongoing currency of URLs.

Printed in China by 1010 Printing International Limited
5 6 7 8 21 20

Cengage Learning Australia
Level 7, 80 Dorcas Street
South Melbourne, Victoria Australia 3205

Cengage Learning New Zealand
Unit 4B Rosedale Office Park
331 Rosedale Road, Albany, North Shore 0632, NZ

For learning solutions, visit **cengage.com.au**

For product information and technology assistance,
in Australia call **1300 790 853**;
in New Zealand call **0800 449 725**

For permission to use material from this text or product, please email
aust.permissions@cengage.com

National Library of Australia Cataloguing-in-Publication Data
Quill, Anne, 1963– author.
Get ahead in grammar : a practical guide for students / Anne Quill, Anne Townsend.
2nd edition.
9780170386166 (paperback)
Includes index.
For secondary school age.
English language--Grammar--Textbooks.
English language--Grammar--Study and teaching (Secondary)
English language--Written English--Textbooks.
English language--Written English--Study and teaching (Secondary)
Written communication.
Townsend, Anne Elizabeth, author.
428.2

INTRODUCTION

What is grammar?

Grammar is a description of a language as a system. In describing a language system, attention is paid to both structure (form) and meaning (function) at the level of a word, a sentence and a text.

THE PURPOSE OF LEARNING ABOUT GRAMMAR AND PUNCTUATION

When learning punctuation and grammar, the Australian Curriculum refers to the importance of:

- **knowing** how grammar is used
- **understanding** grammar in terms of punctuation
- **understanding** how grammar relates to creating, editing and writing
- **understanding** the rules needed for correct usage
- **understanding** how the **purpose** of a text informs the grammar.

This book focuses on the above. It has been written to assist with learning the structures and functions of words and sentences. It uses the metalanguage (e.g. nouns, verbs and similes) of English and shows how it informs the language and contributes to the effectiveness of the text.

When creating texts students learn to appreciate:

i how purpose informs the structure of the text
ii how language is used to create texts that are consistent and coherent.

The graphic below shows how the written text can be broken down. As students become familiar with each section, it will become clear how they relate to the sections above and below.

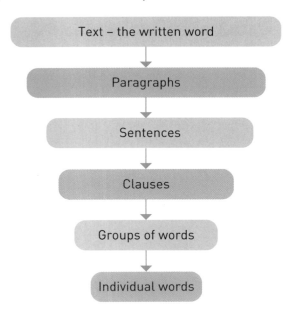

This textbook has been written to meet the standards of the Australian English Curriculum and NAPLAN.

Curriculum grids are available at: www.nelsonsecondary.com.au/getaheadinggrammar

Further information about the structures and functions of text can be found in *Text Types* and *Think Organise Write* by Anne Quill and Anne Townsend.

LANGUAGE ROOTS

Standard Australian English is defined by ACARA as 'the variety of spoken and written English language in Australia used in more formal settings such as for official or public purposes, and recorded in dictionaries, style guides and grammars. While it is always dynamic and evolving, it is recognised as the "common language" of Australians'.

Languages are interrelated and dynamic. The English language has its roots in languages such as Latin and Greek. Knowing this can enhance your understanding of the definitions of the words and how they are used in the language. Understanding language roots can help you to comprehend the meaning of new words and substantially strengthen your vocabulary.

To understand the meanings of new words it is useful to analyse the different parts of the word and their meanings. Prefixes and suffixes are sets of letters that are added to the beginning or end of another word. They are not words in their own right and cannot stand alone in a sentence.

Many new words can be formed by adding a prefix to the beginning of a word. For example, if you add un– to the word 'pleasant' the new word becomes 'unpleasant' meaning 'not pleasant'. If a new word is formed by adding to the end of the word it is called a suffix. Common suffixes are –s and –es meaning 'more than one' and it forms the plural of the word. Adding –es to the word 'lash' changes it to 'lashes' meaning 'more than one lash'.

When the Latin and Greek roots are used as prefixes and suffixes they provide clues to the meaning of the word. In addition, the English language uses words that have their origins connected to other languages such as French and Japanese. For example, there are words that have a French origin such as café, avenue, hospital and bicycle. Words with Japanese origins include bonsai, haiku, manga, karate and judo.

The English language continues to evolve, so recognising that a knowledge of word origins extends your knowledge of vocabulary and spelling is important.

The following page has some examples of Greek and Latin roots and their definition words, showing how they can help with the comprehension of the structures of language. Greek root words often relate to scientific words.

ambi	both	ambiguous, ambidextrous
aqua	water	aquarium, aquamarine
aud	to hear	audience, audition
bene	good	benefit, benevolent
cent	one hundred	century, percent
circum	around	circumference, circumstance
contra/ counter	against	contradict, encounter
dict	to say	dictation, dictator
duc/duct	to lead	conduct, induce
fac	to do; to make	factory, manufacture
form	shape	conform, reform
fort	strength	fortitude, fortress
fract	to break	fracture, fraction
ject	throw	projection, rejection
jud	judge	judicial, prejudice
mal	bad	malevolent, malefactor
mater	mother	material, maternity
mit	to send	transmit, admit
mort	death	mortal, mortician
multi	many	multimedia, multiple
opt	best	optimum, optimal
pater	father	patriarch, paternal
port	carry	portable, import, export
pre	before	predict, previous, prepare

anthropo	man; human; humanity	anthropologist, philanthropy
auto	self	autobiography, automobile
bio	life	biology, biography
chron	time	chronological, chronic
dyna	power	dynamic, dynamite
dys	bad; hard; unlucky	dysfunctional, dyslexic
gram	thing written	epigram, telegram
graph	writing	graphic, phonograph
hetero	different	heteronym, heterogeneous
homo	same	homonym, homogenous
hydr	water	hydration, dehydrate, hydrate
hypo	below; beneath	hypothermia, hypothetical
logy	study of	biology, psychology
meter/ metr	measure	thermometer, perimeter
micro	small	microbe, microscope
mis/miso	hate	misanthrope, misogyny
mono	one	monologue, monotonous
morph	form; shape	morphology, morphing
nym	name	antonym, synonym

CONTENTS

9780170386166

GLOSSARY OF TERMS

The **bold** terms can be found in the text while the green terms provide extra information to complement your understanding of English language terms.

adjective p. 33
a part of speech word that describes a noun and provides information about the noun

adverb p. 31
a part of speech word that describes a verb, adjective or sometimes other adverbs; many adverbs end in –ly

adverbial clause or phrase p. 13
a phrase or clause that gives additional information to the main clause

alliteration p. 6
literary device that uses two or more words with the same beginning consonant sounds placed together for effect

allusion
a reference to a person, event or idea by passing a comment

analogy
a comparison of the similarities between two things, people or situations, often used to persuade, explain or argue a point

apostrophe (') p. 18
a marker used:

* to show that a letter is missing; for example, 'don't'
* to show ownership or possession; for example, 'the boy's cap'.

argument
the reasons and evidence given to support an idea or a proposal

article
a word placed before a noun to form part of the noun group; the English language has three: 'the' is known as the definite article while 'a' and 'an' are the indefinite articles

audience
readers, listeners or viewers who are addressed by a speaker or a writer

auxiliary verb p. 27
a verb that gives further information about a main verb, such as 'be', 'do' and 'have'

bias
preferring one point of view while ignoring or excluding contradictory points of view

brackets p. 19
punctuation markers used to enclose extra information; for example, 'She was in interested in our new political party [Liberal]'

clause p. 12
a group of words containing a subject and a verb, which can form a statement, question, command or exclamation

cohesion
the smooth flow of ideas in a text

cohesive links
language features that help to develop unity within a text, includeing connectives such as 'furthermore' and 'therefore', and pronouns; for example, 'John was going to leave because he had finished his work.'

colon (:) p. 19
Punctuation which often introduces an explanation or is used before a list. The statements that follow the colon do not have to be complete sentences. They may be set out in dot points.

comma (,) p. 19
a punctuation marker used to break up items in list and separate words and phrases at the beginning of or inside a sentence.

command (or imperative) p. 12
a clause structure used when the writer wants to show strong emotion or seeks an active response; commands always end with an exclamation mark; for example, 'Leave now!'

9780170386166

complex sentence p. 9
a sentence that has a main clause and one or more subordinate clauses that depend on the main clause to make sense

compound word
a word consisting of two or more words that has a meaning different from that of the individual word, such as 'farmyard'

comprehension strategies
strategies and processes to find meaning from texts

Key strategies include:

- using prior knowledge
- recognising literal information stated in the text
- making inferences based on information in the text and their own prior knowledge
- predicting what will happen in a text
- summarising and organising information
- joining ideas and information critically reflecting on content, structure, language and images

conjunction p. 35
a word that joins words, phrases or clauses together, such as 'and', 'but', 'so' and 'because'

connective p. 1
words that link paragraphs and sentences together; connectives are important resources for creating cohesion in texts

context
the setting in which a text is created

contraction
a shortened form of one or two words (one of which is usually a verb), where an apostrophe takes the place of the missing letter or letters; for example, 'I'm' (I am), 'can't' (cannot), 'how're' (how are) and 'Ma'am' (Madam)

dash (–) p. 18
a punctuation marker used to indicate the inclusion of more information, a relationship between two things, or a change of thought

digraph
Two letters that represent a single sound (phoneme). Vowel digraphs are two vowels (oo, ea). Consonant digraphs have two consonants (sh, th). Vowel/consonant digraphs have one vowel and one consonant (er, ow).

ellipsis
The omission from speech or writing of a word or words that are superfluous.

embedded clause p. 12
The embedded clause happens within the arrangement of the main clause, e.g. The boy, *who came to visit*, had just moved into the neighbourhood. 'Who came to visit' is the embedded clause.

exclamation mark (!) p. 18
A punctuation marker used at the end of a sentence to show strong emotion or feeling in the sentence, it may be used to strengthen a comical element e.g. 'We found the cat asleep in the laundry tub!'; Sentences containing a command – Go home!

figurative language p. 6
Figurative language uses language that creates an image which conveys more than the literal meaning of the words or phrase. Words or phrases that are used in a non-literal way for particular effect are simile, metaphor, personification. Figurative language may also use elements of other senses such as in hearing with onomatopoeia.

finite verbs p. 27
Verbs that have a specific tense and a subject with which they grammatically agree. A complete sentence must contain a finite verb.

full stop (.) p. 18
a punctuation marker used to indicate the end of a sentence that is a statement or command

e.g. *We will go to the movies.*

gender
nouns, adjectives, verbs and pronouns that must agree when they are referring to males or females.

genre
The categories into which texts are grouped. It is often used to differentiate texts on the basis of their subject matter (detective novels, science fiction and fantasy) or their form and structure (poetry, novels and short stories).

grammar
A description of a language as a system. When describing a language system, it is necessary to take note of both structure (form) and meaning (function) at the level of a word, a sentence and a text.'

grapheme
A letter or a number of letters that represent a sound (phoneme) in a word

e.g. the 'f' in fun, 'ph,'in phantom

homograph p. 4
A word with the same spelling as another, but of different origin and meaning, e.g. *wind* (the wind blows), *wind* (wind the watch).

homonym p. 4
A word with the same sound and the same spelling, but a different meaning, for example *strike* (verb), *strike* (noun).

homophone p. 4
A word with the same sound as another but different spelling and meaning, e.g. *ewe/you*

hyphen (-) p. 18
A punctuation marker used to indicate that a word is divided. The hyphen is placed between syllables or, in the case of compounds, between the parts of the word, e.g. *brother-in-law*

idiom p. 6
a common expression peculiar to an individual or group that cannot be taken literally, e.g. *'Can you lend a hand?'*

irony
a clash between what the words say and what they mean. e.g. Using language that means the opposite 'It was great fun'. *(It was boring)*

a state of affairs or an event that seems deliberately contrary to what one expects and which is amusing as a result.

lexical cohesion
Word associations creating links in texts. They can be made through the use of repetition of words, synonyms, antonyms.

metonymy
The use of the name of one thing or attribute of something to represent something larger.

e.g. the term 9/11 refers to global event

metalanguage
language or system of symbols which can be used to describe and discuss a language

metaphor p. 6
makes a statement that says one thing is another

e.g. *The children are angels.*

My fingers are like blocks of ice.

modality p. 28
The way something exists or is done, having to do with possibility, probability, obligation and permission. Modal meanings can be expressed by the auxiliary verbs 'must' and 'may':

modal verb p. 28
a verb that expresses a degree of probability (e.g. 'I might come back') or a degree of obligation (e.g. 'you must hand it over').

mode
The process of communication: listening, speaking, reading, writing, viewing and representing.

mood
A literary element that evokes certain feelings in readers through words and descriptions. Traditionally classified as indicative (statements and questions), imperative (commands) or subjunctive (hypothetical or conditional). The subjunctive involves use of auxiliaries such as could, may, should, might.

morphemes
the smallest grammatical unit in language

noun p. 21
a word used to represent people, places, ideas and things

noun group p. 21
a group of words built around a noun that describe the noun

onomatopoeia p. 6
using a word that mimics a sound

opinion
Something that is thought to have occurred, existed or believed to be true. When verbalising or writing an opinion, adjectives and adverbs like,' always, ever, should, all, none, good, better, best, tasty, tastier', are most likely to be found. It represents someone's feelings.

parody
a work intended to ridicule or mock the features of another work

persuasive text
used to persuade the reader to agree with a particular point of view

parentheses () p. 18
punctuation markers used to indicate extra information

e.g. *she was reading her new book (Harry Potter).*

personification p. 6
giving human or animate qualities to something that isn't alive

e.g. *The trees sighed and moaned in the wind.*

phonemes
the smallest sound units in a language; building blocks of spoken words

phonemic awareness
The awareness of sounds (phonemes) that make up spoken words which is an important feature of learning to read and spell.

phrase p. 16
a group of related words that has no finite verb

prefix p. iv
a word part that is attached to the beginning of a word to change the meaning

e.g. *un*happy, *dis*like

preposition p. 37
A word that is placed in front of a noun group to indicate where, when, or how an action occurs. It begins an adverbial phrase or an adjectival phrase indicating time, place and manner.

e.g. *in, on, after, before, by, under, over, of, through,*

pronoun p. 25
a word that is used in place of a noun

pronunciation
The way in which a word is pronounced with regard to aspects of articulation.

e.g. stress, intonation pitch, tone and volume

pun
The humorous use of a word or phrase so as to emphasise its different meanings.

prepositional phrases
A preposition followed by a noun or group or phrase

question
a sentence that seeks information, usually added onto a clause in order to signal that a reply or response is required

e.g. *'We will meet tomorrow, won't we?*

question mark (?) p. 18
a punctuation mark used at the end of a sentence to indicate that a question is being asked

quotation marks ('...' or "...") p. 19
* used to indicate a new paragraph and separate quotation marks are used for each speaker being quoted e.g. *'I am feeling sad,' he said.*
* used to indicate the actual words quoted from another source in formal writing
* used to indicate the titles of poems, songs, short stories or articles, e.g *'The Man from Snowy River'*
* used to draw attention to an unusual or particular sense or usage of a word e.g. *Koalas can be 'cranky' creatures.*
* not used for the speech of characters in a drama script.

quoted speech/direct speech
speech in a text giving the exact words that have been spoken; contained with quotation marks

rhetorical device
language that is used in order to persuade an audience by using metaphors, repetition, rhetorical questions

semicolon (;) p. 19
used between independent clauses which are related in meaning. It is used to indicate pauses longer than a comma.

sentence p. 9
a unit of written language consisting of one or more clauses. It begins with a capital letter and ends with a full stop, question mark or exclamation mark. It contains a finite verb.

simile p. 6
compares two dissimilar things. The comparison starts with *like, as* or *as if.*

structure
the arrangement between the component parts

subject p. 10
A person or thing that is being discussed or described. It is usually filled by a noun group.
e.g. *The unhappy girl (subject) was crying.*

subject–verb agreement
The form of the verb must agree with the number of its subject, a noun or noun group.
e.g. *The children were not at school.*

suffix
word part that is attached to the end of a word to change the meaning or form, f
e.g. 'contain*er*.'

synonym p. 4
two words with similar meanings
e.g. *affection – fondness*

syntax
the way in which sentences and clauses are structured. They are divided into subject, verb and object,
e.g. *'James (subject) pointed (verb) his finger (object)'.*

tense p. 29
tell us whether an action occurred in the past *[past tense]*, is occurring now *[present tense]* or will occur in the future *[future tense]*

text connectives p. 1
join clauses together in a sentence, and then join sentences in a long piece and often called conjunctions

texts
The main body of a book or other piece of writing, as distinct from other material such as notes, appendices, and illustrations. They can be written, spoken, non-verbal, visual or multimodal.

text structures
A way in which information is organised, for example, by chapter headings, subheadings, tables of contents, indexes and glossaries, overviews, introductory and concluding paragraphs, sequencing, topic sentences, taxonomies and cause and effect.

theme
refers to the main idea or message of a text

types of text
can be imaginative, informative or narrative

verb p. 27
an action word that describes what is happening in the sentence

verb group p. 27
a combination of verbs

word chain p. 4
a sequence of nouns and noun groups or verbs and verb groups that link text to a particular content.

word origin [etymology]
the source and history of a word, e.g *photograph* from the Greek words for 'light' and picture

writing
composing a text for publication in written form

GRAMMAR AT THE TEXT LEVEL

CONNECTIVES

A **connective** can join two sentences or two paragraphs together.

TYPES OF CONNECTIVES

- time
- cause
- addition
- contrast

PURPOSE

To link:
- two sentences to make a paragraph in order to develop ideas
- one paragraph to another.

STRUCTURE	HOW CONNECTIVES ARE USED
Time • Sequence of events: *first, next, soon, afterwards, finally* • Two events take place at different times: *earlier, until then* • Two events happen at the same time: *meanwhile, at the same time*	They felt happy to see their friends come into sight. *Until then* they had been worried for their safety. You do the shopping; *meanwhile*, I'll do the cleaning and the washing.
Cause and result • An event has occurred: *therefore, as a result, consequently* • The reason why: *because of, so that, due to* • Inference: *otherwise, in that case* • It is a condition: *as long as, considering that*	The boys had been training hard for this event for many months and, *as a result*, they won a gold medal for their country. You can go to the party *as long as* you are home by midnight.

STRUCTURE	HOW CONNECTIVES ARE USED
Addition • It is of equal importance: *besides, moreover, furthermore, similarly, as well* • Explaining something in another way or in more detail: *namely, that is* • Adding the example: *for example* • Summing up: *in conclusion, therefore, in fact, overall*	He had read all he could find on the history of Chinese culture. *Furthermore*, he had also travelled extensively in China over the last 20 years. All the students in the swimming team, *namely* John, Chrissie, Ryan and Leah, have to go to the pool at lunchtime.
Contrast • Contrast: *on the other hand, yet, rather, but* • It is an alternative: *however, rather than, alternatively* • Comparing: *in comparison, in contrast, likewise* • Conceding: *however, though, in any case, despite that, anyhow*	It was cold, *yet* she wasn't wearing a coat. His argument supported his team's case. *However*, he knew that the opposition would put forward a totally different point of view.

PARAGRAPHS

DEFINITION

A **paragraph** contains a main or topic sentence followed by a number of supporting ideas.

TYPES OF PARAGRAPHS

- narrative
- descriptive
- informative

PURPOSE

- to tell a story – narrative
- to describe a person place or thing – descriptive
- to gives information about a person, place or thing – informative

Use of different types of paragraphs can enhance a text.

Example: Paragraphs and connectives Text type: Narrative

WATER STORY

The Bryson family lived on a property in western NSW. There were four boys in the family and, as they grew up, their love and commitment to the land was as intense as that of their parents.

> Each *paragraph* begins with a topic sentence and contains sentences supporting the main idea.

However, one day they heard their parents talking about selling the property and they were amazed.

> *Connective* indicating an alternative idea

Their land consisted of a large tract that was used to grow a variety of crops and to run cattle. It was bordered by a fast-flowing river that in previous times had provided them with the water needed for the survival of the crops and their animals. The river had high banks and the water was fresh and clear. A thick border of native trees provided shelter and food for the native birds and animals. In recent months, the farms upstream were using a much greater amount of the water. Consequently, the family faced an impossible situation. Without adequate water supplies they would not be able to continue.

> Each *paragraph* tells a story.
>
> Each *paragraph* describes a person place or thing.
>
> Each *paragraph* gives information about a person, place or thing.
> *Connective* showing result

A water-sharing plan was then proposed so that those who lived further down the river were sure of a fair amount of water. Farmers would be allocated water shares according to their needs. If some shares were not used, they could be passed them on to those who were needier.

With the support of all, the scheme was introduced immediately. Therefore, there was no longer any need to talk of selling and the family could look forward to a much brighter and secure future.

> The last *paragraph* concludes the story.
>
> *Connective* showing result

DEFINITION

A **word chain** is a series of different nouns/noun groups or verbs/verb groups that link a text together by describing the same content.

TYPES OF WORD CHAINS

- synonyms
- antonyms
- homonyms
- homophones

PURPOSE

- *synonyms:* two words that have similar meaning
- *antonyms:* two words that have opposite meanings
- *homonyms:* two words that sound the same and are spelled the same but have a different meaning
- *homophones:* two words that sound the same but have a different meaning and spelling
- *homograph:* two words that are spelled the same but have a different sound and meaning

STRUCTURE	HOW WORD CHAINS ARE USED
Synonyms: • can be found in a thesaurus.	Synonyms for **affection:** *love, liking, fondness, warmth*
Antonyms: • can be found in a thesaurus • are often formed by adding a prefix such as *un, in, ir, im* and *dis* • can also be formed by changing the prefix or suffix.	comfortable *uncomfortable* settled *unsettled* responsible *irresponsible* reversible *irreversible* capable *incapable* competent *incompetent* possible *impossible* patient *impatient* increase *decrease* internal *external* useful *useless* careful *careless*
Homonyms: • look and sound like the same word but have a different meaning and origin • are learnt unconsciously by native speakers of English but often confuse those learning the language • are named for the Greek 'homo' (same) and 'nym' (name)	suit *suit* scale *scale* round *round* ground *ground*
Homophones: • sound the same but have a different meaning and spelling • are named for the Greek 'homo' (same) and 'phone' (sound)	addition *edition* knew *new* male *mail* dear *deer*
Homographs: • have the same spelling but sound different, with a different meaning and origin • are named for the Greek 'homo' (same) and 'graph' (write)	wind – *wind* (same sound as why) minute – *minute* (same sound as my newt) lead – *lead* (same sound as head)

WORD CHAINS

Example: Word chains   **Text type:** Information report

ENOGGERA CREEK

The headwaters of Enoggera Creek are in the D'Aguilar Ranges near Mt Nebo. The creek flows down between the ranges through many suburbs on its journey to the sea.

This report aims to determine the health of the creek and the effect of the introduction of non-native flora, domestic run-off and pollution.

Many specimens of native flora and fauna in the creek area have disappeared. Trees have been cut down and this has reduced the number of animals who can live in the area because of the lack of protection or food sources. When we compare present photos with those of the past, we see that the previous diversity of plant and animal life no longer exists. Local residents have used the banks for disposal of garden clippings and introduced species of plants have taken over the native fauna.

Water tests that have been carried out have shown that there is now a high level of toxicity in the creek. There are many factories along the banks and their waste products may be leaching into the water. This has reduced the numbers of native fish that can be sustained in the creek.

Residents often sight waste products and rubbish in the creek. These can cause injury or death to the animals and fish if they become tangled in plastic bags or cans.

Our findings would suggest that there is significant evidence of pollution at this site.

One solution would be to lobby council to impose more penalties on organisations that allow waste products to leach into the creek.

Local residents should also be made more aware of the problems caused by the disposal of their garden rubbish and be urged to support clean-up days.

Antonyms

past – present

native – non-native

health – injury; death; toxicity

pollution – clean up

Synonyms

toxicity – pollution

pollution – run-off

waste products – garden clippings; rubbish

Homonyms

sight – site

Homophones

can – can(s)

FIGURATIVE LANGUAGE

DEFINITION

Figurative language is used to create an image that conveys more than the literal meaning of the words or phrase.

TYPES OF FIGURATIVE LANGUAGE

- creative word play: alliteration, onomatopoeia
- simile
- metaphor
- personification

- evaluative language
- idiom
- sensory language: sight, smell, touch and sound words
- repetition

PURPOSE

The purpose of figurative language is to enhance the text.

CONTEXT

- is used in poetry, fiction and everyday speech
- ranges in complexity from a literal explanation to a figure of speech.

STRUCTURE	HOW FIGURATIVE LANGUAGE IS USED
Alliteration refers to two words together with the same beginning consonant sound.	**S**even **s**lippery **s**nakes **s**lipped by.
Onomatopoeia means using a word that makes a sound.	The water *splashed* onto the bank. The wind *whistled* through the trees.
A **simile** compares two unlike things using the words *like* or *as*.	The pelican came in to land *like a plane* in descent. The burglar moved *as silently as a cat* through the house.
A **metaphor** makes a statement that says one thing is another.	The children *are angels*. He *was a tower of strength*.
Personification means to give human or animate qualities to something that is not alive.	The flames of the fire *licked* at the edge of the house.
Evaluative language judges an action or event.	He made an *excellent* choice. Without a job, her future seemed *bleak*.
An **idiom** is a common expression peculiar to an individual or a group.	*couch potato* *you're kidding* *know it all* *cool* *lend a hand* *radical*
Sensory language means words related to smell, sight, touch and sound.	His shoes *crunched* the *brittle* grass as he moved towards the crease, bat in *padded* hand, ready to *crush* the opposing team.
Repetition uses the same word deliberately, for emphasis.	He *hoped* to return. He *hoped* to see his parents again. He *hoped*.

Example: Figurative language

Text type: Poetry – free verse

THE STORM

Threatening the earth

    obscuring sunlight

Black clouds ever darkening

    convulsing

like the mixer of life

    moving at speed

shafts of lightning

    shooting downward

like shards of glass

    exploding with force

earth eagerly expecting

    wild precipitation

deluge delivered

    thankfulness

energy to the earth

    up and running

alliteration: deluge delivered *(the sound of the letter 'd' emphasises the force of the rain)*

onomatopoeia: exploding *(provides an image of the intensity and force of the lightning)*

simile: like shards of glass; like the mixer of life *(likens shafts of lightening to shards of glass and compares black clouds to how our own life can become turbulent and complicated)*

sensory language: shafts of lightning shooting downward *(describes what can be seen)*

personification: black clouds … convulsing *(conjures an image of a convulsing person, not in control of their body)*

evaluative: thankfulness *(evaluates the deluge and its contribution to the environment)*

idiom: up and running *(reminds us how important the rain is and that it brings an opportunity to start again)*

Example: Figurative language   Text type: Narrative

THE PIANO EXAM

I heard Mum say that I'd got out of bed on the wrong side this morning, just because I was shouting at everyone. You see today I sat for my first piano exam. Scared was how I felt!

Mum and I arrived at the venue for the test; it seemed as quiet as a graveyard. I had so many competing thoughts tossing around in my head. Would the piano be my friend? How did I address the examiner? 'Good morning, Your Highness' or 'Hello, my Lord.' We settled on a simple, 'Good morning,' as we waited outside the studio.

A kindly lady appeared and after picking proudly through her plentiful papers directed me to the practice room. She suggested a pre-exam practice to settle my nerves.

A little later she returned to lead me into the exam room. My examiner looked very posh in a brown-checked suit and smelled of Dad's aftershave. I heard him say, 'Nothing to be nervous about'. Easy for him! As I sat down my heart was pounding. All I could hear was thump, bang, thump, bang. Even the piano was scared! How would he hear my playing? I wondered.

Two weeks later I received my results. My knees were jelly as I tore open the envelope. I had passed.

Now to relax, until next year …

Alliteration: picking proudly; plentiful papers

Idiom: got out of bed on the wrong side

simile: as quiet as a graveyard *(not a sound can be heard)*

Personification: Would the piano be my friend?
Even the piano was scared!

Sensory language: … looked very posh in a brown-checked suit and smelled of Dad's aftershave.

Onomatopoeia: thump, bang, thump, bang *(words that make a sound)*

Metaphor: My knees were jelly *(wobbly with fear)*

GRAMMAR AT THE SENTENCE LEVEL

SENTENCES

DEFINITION

A **sentence**:
- is written in the context of a piece of text
- has a finite verb
- has a subject and a predicate.

TYPES OF SENTENCES
- *simple:* made up of a group of words that have a finite verb
- *compound:* made up of two or more main clauses joined by a conjunction.
- *complex:* has a main clause and one or more subordinate clauses that depend on the main clause to make sense.

PURPOSE
- The purpose of a simple sentence is to express a complete thought.
- Compound and complex sentences can add to the mystery of the text by building a sense of suspense. They provide more depth to the content and are used to create more interesting texts by adding to the complexity of the text.

SENTENCES

STRUCTURE	HOW SIMPLE SENTENCES ARE USED
A simple sentence ────────→ A simple sentence contains: • an expression of a complete thought • one verb • two parts – the subject and the predicate. The subject is the name of a person or thing. To find the subject, we can ask who or what *ate* and the answer is *the boy*. The predicate tells us about the person or thing (the subject). To find the predicate we can ask what the boy did and the answer is *ate the hamburger*.	*The boy ate the hamburger. (simple sentence)* *ate (verb)* *The boy (subject)* *ate the hamburger (predicate)*

STRUCTURE	HOW COMPOUND SENTENCES ARE USED
A compound sentence ────────→ A compound sentence contains: • two main clauses • two finite verbs such as *went* and *saw* • a conjunction that joins the clauses, such as *and*, *but* or *so*.	*The children went for a walk and they saw many exciting things.* The children *went* for a walk *(clause 1)* *and (conjunction)* They *saw* many exciting things. *(clause 2)*

STRUCTURE	HOW COMPLEX SENTENCES ARE USED
A complex sentence ────────→ A complex sentence contains: • a main clause • a subordinate clause that is dependent on the main clause, which means that one thing could not have happened without the other. A subordinate clause begins with words such as *so*, *when*, *which*, *while*, *who*, *what*, *although*, *if*, *until*, *as* and *because*.	*The students saw many interesting aspects of Aboriginal culture when they went on their excursion.* The students saw many interesting aspects of Aboriginal culture... *(main clause)* ...*when* they went on their excursion. *(subordinate clause)* saw, went *(finite verbs)*

SENTENCES

Example: Sentences   Text type: Narrative

THE PREY

It was time for school. Leon had just turned off his favourite TV program. As he paused to go up the stairs, he glanced out of the window. Something caught his eye. He caught a glimpse of her sliding steadily along the side of the path.

The sunlight shone through the trees and it cast dark shadows. Glancing nervously about, she kept to the grass. She moved as if she were trying to escape from something. *Then she slithered across to the other side so that she would remain hidden in the taller grasses.*

There was movement among the shadows of the trees; something was following her without the slightest sound. *She could not see it but she knew that it was there. Her heart began to race.*

The predator was beginning to lose patience. He saw his chance so he flew ahead of her. He perched in a small tree that was blocking the sunlight, poised and ready to swoop.

Below him she hesitated, but too late. As she slid under the tree he swooped and in one quick movement her life was over.

Marty ran to tell his mum what he had seen from the window.

'Well when you think of it, I suppose you could say that the kookaburra was lucky to have such a special treat for breakfast,' she commented.

Simple sentences

It was time for school.

Her heart began to race.

Compound sentences

The sunlight shone through the trees and it cast dark shadows.

She could not see it but she knew that it was there. *[Each sentence builds the suspense.]*

Complex sentences

Then she slithered across to the other side so that she would remain hidden in the taller grasses.

'Well when you think of it, I suppose you could say that the kookaburra was lucky to have such a special treat for breakfast,' she commented.

GRAMMAR AT THE CLAUSE LEVEL

CLAUSES

Clauses are groups of words that include a subject and a verb. Clauses can form a:
- statement
- question
- command
- exclamation.

- main or principal
- subordinate
  - adverbial
  - adjectival
- noun
- embedded

A **main clause** tells us about an action and those involved in the action. It makes sense by itself. It contains a subject and a verb.

A **subordinate clause** adds more information and meaning to the main clause, but it does not make sense by itself. It contains a subject and a verb.

An **embedded clause** is a clause that occurs within the structure of the main clause and is usually marked by commas. Information related to the sentence topic is put into the middle of the sentence to give the reader more information and enhance the sentence; for example, 'The boys *who came to play* were friends of my son.'

- Clauses can stand alone as simple sentences.
- Clauses can be combined to make compound and complex sentences.

CLAUSES

STRUCTURE	HOW CLAUSES ARE USED
Main [principal] clause: • makes sense by itself • can stand alone.	The children swam in the sea.
Subordinate clause: • adds more information to the main clause • depends on the main clause because it needs the principal clause to make sense • can be adverbial, adjectival or noun clauses.	*Principal clause* The children swam in the sea *while their parents sat on the sand.* *Subordinate clause*
Adverbial clause: • does the work of an adverb by describing the how, when, where and why about a verb • begins with *as, although, if, as....as, so, because, after, until, while, how, when, where* or *why.*	• He will do *as* he pleases. *(how)* • She came *when* she heard him call. *(when)* • They sat *where* they could see the game. *(where)* • I love to visit my aunty *because* she gives me ice cream. *(why)*
Adjectival clause: • does the work of an adjective and gives more information about the noun • begins with *who, whom, which* or *that.*	• She chatted with the man *who was watching the tennis.* • The mountain, *which we wanted to climb, was very high*. • She indicated to the *boy to whom she had been speaking*, to leave the room.
Noun clause: • does the work of the noun and can be either the subject or the object of the verb • can begin with a conjunction, such as *what, that, if* or *whether.*	• *Whether John knows the girl* is not important. *(subject)* • They ignored *what he had said. (object)*
Embedded clause: • is a clause contained within a nother clause in order to give more information and enhance the sentence • is often marked by commas.	The children *who had been invited to the party* were meeting in the park. Many of the animals, *who were in restrictive cages*, had come from the freedom of the wild.

Example: Clauses   Text type: Narrative

WILD RIDE

Becoming a member of a cool bike group seemed to be an exciting challenge. *James wanted to join this group*, but there was one problem. *The leader had informed him that he had to do something 'cool' to become a member*. Not wanting them to think that he was at all scared, he had readily agreed. That had been the easy part. Now he had to think of what to do!

He decided to search the big shed at the back of his *house that concealed many old and interesting things*. As he rummaged around, he found something big and bulky under an old blanket. As he lifted the blanket away, he was amazed. He had found a unicycle. The previous owners of the house *who had been part of a circus troop* must have left it. *If he was able to ride it along the main street of the town*, he was sure that the gang members would be impressed.

Each afternoon he rushed home from school and began his practice sessions. As the week progressed, he was beginning to balance quite well. He had until Saturday to perfect his riding.

The day arrived and he met up with the gang at the top of Main Street. Initially they were most impressed.

'Wow,' said Johnnie. 'I've never seen anyone ride one of these – especially down that hill!'

That was a compliment coming from the leader. Still James felt sick inside *when he heard this comment*. His plan had been to ride on the flat part of the street not downhill. As he followed Johnnie's gaze to where Main Street fell away sharply, he was aghast! However, *although he was terrified*, he wanted to impress the gang.

'Scared are you, James?' taunted gang members Ozzie and Leo, looking so cool in their black leather jackets and sunglasses.

Main clause

James wanted to join this group ...

The leader had informed him ...

Subordinate clause

... that he had to do something 'cool' to become a member. *(helps us to understand more about the challenge)*

Adjectival clause

... that concealed many old and interesting things *(gives more information about the house)*

Embedded clause

... who had been part of a circus troop ...

Adverbial clause of condition

If he was able to ride it along the main street of the town ...

Adverbial clause of time

... when he heard this comment.

Adverbial clause of concession

although he was terrified ... *(regardless of how he felt he had to impress the gang)*

Example: Clauses   Text type: Narrative

'Go!' shouted the boys. Before James knew what was happening, he was off. Balancing well, he gathered momentum as he headed down towards the hill. He was feeling quite proud of himself until it dawned on him *that he would have to negotiate a tight turn without brakes*. As he gathered speed, he could see that the road levelled out a little and he might be able to turn in that spot and somersault onto the soft lawn of the local park. Before he knew it, he was soaring through the air and then he landed with a soft thud.

The gang had been watching with mouths wide open in amazement. *What they had seen* had been fantastic!

'That was just the best James!' they shouted.

Although he had passed the coolness test, he wasn't sure that joining the gang was all he wanted. Maybe he could join the circus instead!

Noun clause

... that he would have to negotiate a tight turn without brakes.
(Answers the question: What had dawned on him?)

What they had seen ...
(Answers the question: What had been fantastic?)

PHRASES

DEFINITION

A **phrase**:
- is a group of related words that has no finite verb.
- can be part of a sentence.
- usually contains words that relate to each other.

TYPES OF PHRASES

- adjectival
- adverbial
- noun

PURPOSE

It is used in a sentence to make the sentence more interesting.

STRUCTURE	HOW PHRASES ARE USED
An adjectival phrase: • works like an adjective by describing a noun or pronoun and giving it more meaning.	That girl *in the red dress* is a friend of mine. *(describes the girl's appearance)*
An adverbial phrase: • works like an adverb by adding more meaning to the action of the verb • tells us how, when, where or why an action takes place.	The boys were playing cricket *on the grassy oval*. *(tells where the boys were playing)*

9780170386166

PHRASES

STRUCTURE	HOW PHRASES ARE USED
A noun phrase: • works like a noun and takes the place of a noun • includes a noun and one or more modifying words, such as an adjective, an adverb or a preposition.	*Playing cricket* is fun for adults and children. *(Question: What is fun?* *Answer: playing cricket.* *The phrase acts like a noun and begins with the verbal noun or gerund, **playing**.)*
Adding phrases: • can improve your writing by creating a more descriptive picture.	A dog ... A *dangerous looking* dog ... A *dangerous looking* dog *standing over the helpless victim* ...

Example: Phrases   Text type: Explanation

CRICKET

Playing sport is one of the most popular leisure activities in Australia and cricket is one of the most popular games. Young and old, male and female players in cities as well as rural areas, all enjoy cricket.

Two teams of eleven players are needed. The aim of the game is to bowl out the other team before they reach the run total of the opposing team. Each side usually bats and bowls twice. These sessions are called 'innings'. To begin the game, the umpire tosses a coin and each captain calls 'heads' or 'tails'. Of course, only one can win this toss, so the captain who wins can choose to bat or field first.

One team fields while the other team bats. The batting side tries to get as many runs as possible. Different shots earn different scores. For example, if the batter hits the ball *over the fence* without it touching the ground on its way out, this is called a 'six' and six runs are awarded to that player.

There are many ways of getting 'out', including catching the batter's ball *on the full* or knocking over the stumps behind the batter. Not every player in the fielding team will bowl. Bowling is reserved for specialist players; for example, a 'leg-spinner' or a 'pace' bowler.

When all players in the batting side are 'out', the fielding side becomes the batting side and vice versa. The new batting side will try to get more runs than the other side before being bowled out. *The new fielding* side will try to bowl out the batting side or 'get wickets', before they reach the run total.

Noun phrase

Playing sport *(more descriptive than just sport)*

Noun phrase

Two teams of eleven players ... *(noun = teams; modified by of eleven players)*

Adverbial phrase

over the fence *(describes where the ball was hit)*

Adverbial phrase

on the full *(describes how to get 'out')*

Adjectival phrase

The new fielding *(describes the noun side)*

DEFINITION

Punctuation is the use of marks and signs in writing and printing, to separate words into sentences, clauses and phrases in order to make the meaning clear.

TYPES OF PUNCTUATION MARKS

- full stop .
- question mark ?
- exclamation mark or point !
- comma ,
- semicolon ;
- colon :
- apostrophe ʼ
- quotation marks " "
- brackets [ ] or parentheses ( ).

PURPOSE

The purpose of punctuation is to assist the reading process and allow it to move along smoothly. Lack of punctuation can create confusion.

STRUCTURE	HOW PUNCTUATION MARKS ARE USED
Full stops are used: • at the end of a sentence • in abbreviations.	They went to see the animals at the Zoo. N.S.W.
Question marks are used: • at the end of a sentence that asks a question • in direct speech when a question is asked.	How are you going to school? "Who owns that basketball?" asked the teacher.
Exclamation marks are used: • when the writer wants to show strong emotion e.g. excitement, anger, surprise or disappointment.	What a wonderful surprise! Ouch!
Apostrophes: • show that a letter is missing • show ownership i.e. an apostrophe is placed after the last letter of the owner.	don't; can't; wouldn't the boy's cap; the student's books; the teachers' classes
Hyphens: • link two or more words or word parts.	brother-in-law; co-operate
Dashes: • include more information • indicate a change of thought.	The sunset was glorious – a soft, golden rose colour. This is my decision – I am not sure about you – but I have to leave.

9780170386166

PUNCTUATION

STRUCTURE	HOW PUNCTUATION MARKS ARE USED
Commas are used: • to break up the items of a list *When and occurs before the last item there is no need for a comma.* • to separate the words, phrases and clauses at the beginning of a sentence • to separate the words, phrases and clauses inside a sentence • when two or more adjectives are used to modify a noun; or two or more adverbs are used to modify a verb.	Cassie had a teddy bear, a doll, a tea set and a soft pillow in her toy box. At daylight, we set off for the trip to the mountains. I let my pet bird, Aussie, fly around the room. Leila was a bright, cheerful student. The snake wriggled slowly, silently and carefully towards its prey.
Commas in direct speech: • are used at the end of a statement before the speech marks • are used when a statement is interrupted by the words used to explain direct speech.	'I am feeling happy,' she said. 'I am not ready,' he said, 'to participate in that competition.'
Quotation marks: • are used to indicate direct speech • are used to indicate either quoted words or words used with special significance • titles require quotation marks • a direct quotation from an author should be enclosed in quotation marks and give the author name, date and page number(s) that the quotation was taken from, in parentheses.	'Let's go out for the day,' said Mum. It's supposed to be 'a working holiday' but you haven't done any work yet and you've been on holiday for three months! My favourite book is 'Harry Potter.' My favourite proverb is "A rolling stone gathers no moss." "Language is subject to change, and is not caused by unnecessary sloppiness, laziness or ignorance" (Aitchison, 1981, p.67).
Colon: • often introduces an explanation or a series of examples • is used before a list with or without dot points.	To succeed you need: hard work, thoroughness and luck. Items to be taken to camp: • sleeping bag • towels • pillow • clothes for three days.
Brackets or parentheses: • are used to enclose extra information.	• sneakers [old; for walking in the creek]
Semicolon: • is used between independent clauses which are related in meaning • is used to indicate pauses longer than a comma.	I am going home; I intend to stay there.

Example: Punctuation   Text type: News Report

PILOT'S PREDICAMENT

Airport security and fire brigades were on stand-by last night when a flight from Cairns signalled to the airport staff that they were having trouble with their landing gear. The pilot reported that he was unsure about the safety of the landing gear on his aircraft. According to the information from his control panel, it appeared that there had been a problem with the machinery that locked in the landing wheels.

Staff at the airport suggested that flying over the control tower might help them to establish whether the wheels were in place. After an inspection from below, they decided that the wheels looked safe. However to avoid any risk, the aircraft was instructed to go out to sea to jettison its fuel. The crew prepared the passengers for an emergency landing. All procedures were put into place and the aircraft made its landing safely.

Later, a spokesperson for the company reported that there had been a fault within the control panel. When the pilot was interviewed, he had nothing but praise for the staff and crew who had supported him throughout the ordeal.

"Thank God we landed safely," he said, "I was relieved to be able to put the aircraft down without having to make an emergency landing."

Apostrophe: shows ownership i.e. the predicament belonged to the pilot

Hyphen: links two words

Capital letter: begins every sentence

Full stop: ends every sentence

Comma: separates parts of a sentence

Quotation marks: indicate direct speech

NOUNS AND NOUN GROUPS

DEFINITION

A **noun** is a naming word used to represent a person, place or thing.

TYPES OF NOUNS

- proper
- collective
- concrete
- abstract
- technical
- terms of address
- nominalisation
- singular, plural
- countable
- uncountable

PURPOSE

A **noun** may be used as a subject of a **sentence**, as a direct object, as an indirect object, or it may be used as the object of a preposition.

CONTEXT

- A *proper noun* is used to name a person, place or thing; it begins with a capital letter.
- A *common noun* is a noun referring to a person, place or thing in a general sense. It is written with a capital letter only when it begins a sentence.
- A *collective noun* is the name for a group of individual people or things. A collective noun refers to the group as one single unit and it is important to remember this so that the correct verb is used (i.e. may be singular not plural).
- A *concrete noun* is a noun which names anything that can be perceived through the physical senses: touch, sight, taste, hearing, or smell.
- An *abstract noun* is the name for an intangible object i.e. an object which can't be perceived through the senses.
- A *technical noun* is the name used for a technical term.
- *Terms of address* are also nouns.
- *Nominalisation* is the process of forming a noun from a verb. It creates variety and prevents repetition of the verb. It is a useful skill as it conveys an impersonal tone.
- *Noun groups* are groups of words telling who or what is involved in an action to give more information about the noun. They may occur in place of the subject or the object of the verb. They can link different articles, adjectives and nouns together.

STRUCTURE	HOW NOUNS ARE USED
Proper nouns: • always start with a capital letter • names of people • names of places • names of days, months • names of products like books, poems, plays, songs	• Bill, Fred, Jacob, Captain Jones • Australia, Ashgrove • Monday, March • *The Lion the Witch and the Wardrobe, True Blue, The Man from Snowy River*
Common nouns. are everyday names for objects.	room, skateboard, friend, boy, hat
Collective nouns. are names for groups of things.	class, herd, litter, team, band, pack
Concrete nouns. are names for tangible objects.	perfume, beach, dog, noise
Abstract nouns. are names for ideas that cannot be seen or touched.	hope, love, joy, speed, beauty, kindness
Technical nouns. are names for technical terms.	theodolite, rhombus, tetrahedron
Terms of address. include Mr, Mrs, Ms, Dr, Senator, President.	Dr Morrison
Nominalisation. forming a noun from a verb or adjective.	Cancer *is increasing* steadily and doctors **are becoming** *concerned*. *(verb, adjective)* The steady *increase* in cancer is causing *concern* among doctors. *(nouns)*
Noun groups. • groups of words telling who or what is involved in an action. • can include adjectival phrases • can include adjectival clauses • can have more than one noun.	*The run-down old building* is for sale. *The building with the broken gate* is for sale. The building *that we saw today* is for sale. *Peter and Paul* are brothers.

NOUNS - SINGULAR AND PLURAL

Nouns can be *singular* (meaning one) or *plural* (meaning more than one). Check your dictionary if you are not sure of a plural spelling.

Plurals are formed in various ways.

SINGULAR FORM	HOW TO FORM THE PLURAL	PLURAL FORM
coat	Add *s* to make the plural.	coats
beach, fox, bus, wish, business, church	Add *es* to make the plural.	beaches, foxes, buses, wishes, businesses, churches
pony, baby, lady	When the noun ends in *y* and has a consonant before the *y*, drop the *y* and add *ies*.	ponies, babies, ladies
knife, thief	When nouns end in *f* or *fe*, change to *ves*.	knives, thieves
tomato, potato	Add *es* if final *o* comes after a consonant.	tomatoes, potatoes
man, crisis	Change an internal vowel.	men, crises
mouse	Change an internal consonant and vowel.	mice
child, ox	Add *en* or *ren*.	children, oxen
sheep, deer, trout	No change from the singular to the plural form.	sheep, deer, trout
spoonful, sister-in-law	Compound nouns are made up of two words. To form the plural add s to the end of the word or add s to the first part of the compound for hyphenated words.	spoonfuls, sisters-in-law
formula, medium, plateau	Noun endings can change completely.	formulae, media, plateaux

Example: Nouns   Text type: Recount

VISITING KURNELL

On Wednesday, we went to Kurnell to visit Captain Cook's landing place in Australia.

We travelled by bus leaving at 9.30am and arriving at 10.00am. During the journey everyone felt very excited and we interviewed some of our students to record how they were feeling.

At Kurnell we saw a monument to Captain Cook and his crew. I was surprised at the size of the statues and how real they looked. Some took photos to use in their journals.

The beauty of the area amazed us. While we were having morning tea, we sat in an area that gave us a spectacular view of the bay. We saw huge container ships leaving their anchorage and wondered what cargo they were carrying to distant countries.

We went for a bushwalk along the Muru Trail. Along the way we saw a variety of banksias including Golden Banksia and Old Man Banksia. As the trail progressed, we noticed enormous termite nests in the trees. Part of the track led us across a long low wooden bridge that spanned the rippling water of a creek. The beauty of this area was breathtaking. Eventually the path wound round to the place where our bus was waiting for us.

The increase in the numbers of visitors to this area has been astounding. I hope they continue to respect the environment and keep its present pristine condition.

After a long journey back we arrived a tired but happy group

What a great day it had been!

Proper nouns
Wednesday
Kurnell
Cook
Australia
Muru Trail
Golden Banksia
Old Man Banksia

Common nouns
tea
area
bay
cargo
countries

Plural nouns
statues
photos
journals

Singular nouns
track
bridge
creek
path

Collective nouns
crew
group

Abstract nouns
beauty
kindness
view

Technical noun
anchorage

Term of address
Captain

Nominalisation
increase (the verb to *increase* is used as a noun)

PRONOUNS

DEFINITION

A **pronoun** is used in place of a noun so that the idea can be repeated without repeating the noun.

TYPES OF PRONOUNS

Personal, possessive, relative, demonstrative, indefinite, reflexive, interrogative.

PURPOSE

The purpose is to replace a noun to provide a variety of expression. It makes the text more interesting and helps it to flow.

CONTEXT

- A personal pronoun is used in place of a person's name or title.
- A possessive pronoun shows ownership.
- A relative pronoun is used when we refer to animals, places or things.
- A demonstrative pronoun stands for the noun.
- An indefinite pronoun does not refer to anything in particular.
- A reflexive pronoun is made when we add -self or -selves (plural) to the personal pronoun.
- An interrogative pronoun is used to ask a question.

STRUCTURE	HOW PRONOUNS ARE USED	PRONOUN FORMS
A **personal** pronoun is used instead of repeating the noun. It can be singular or plural.	*Bill* had his lunch. *He* was feeling hungry.	**Singular:** I, you, he/ she/ it, me, you, her/ him/ it **Plural:** we, you, they, us, you, them
A **possessive** pronoun shows ownership. It can be singular or plural.	This apple is *mine*. The chocolates were *theirs*.	**Singular:** mine, yours, his/ hers/its **Plural:** ours, yours, theirs
A **relative** pronoun stands instead of the noun.	This is the *book that* he is reading. *Jim, who* was reading the book, looked up.	who, whom, that, which
A **demonstrative** pronoun stands for the noun.	That computer over there belongs to the school. *This* is mine.	this, that, these, those
An **indefinite** pronoun will include *body* or *one* if it is referring to a person; and *thing* if referring to a thing.	This news is for *everybody*. They have to pick up *everything*.	one, none, someone, somebody, something, everyone, everybody, everything, anyone, anything, anybody

STRUCTURE	HOW PRONOUNS ARE USED	PRONOUN FORMS
A **reflexive** pronoun is created by adding *self* or *selves* to a personal pronoun.	She collected the papers *herself*. 'Dry *yourselves* when you get out of the pool,' the teacher told the swimming class.	**Singular:** myself, yourself, herself, himself, itself **Plural:** ourselves, yourselves, themselves
An **interrogative** pronoun is used to ask questions.	*Which* boy finished first?	who, whose, whom, which, what

Example: Pronouns   Text type: Description

WHO IS COCO?

Coco spends *his* life entertaining. *He* is a clown *who* loves to make children laugh. Before each show, *he* spends at least an hour putting on *his* make-up.

Firstly *he* covers *his* face with white paint. Next come the big soulful eyes and circles of red on *his* cheeks. Underneath each eye there is a large teardrop, *which* gives *him* such a sad appearance. Black arched eyebrows enhance *his* expression. *His* lips are drawn heavily with bright pink lipstick and to all of this *he* adds *his* bright red nose.

His clothes are colourful. On *his* head, *his* bright red curly wig is topped with a smart black top hat decorated with a yellow rose. *His* baggy clown suit is white with blue spots and has large red pompoms down the front. People wonder how *he* manages to walk in shoes that are shiny black, have large purple bows and are twice the length of *his* feet.

During each show the children become transfixed. *Their* eyes follow *him* around the ring. *Everyone* laughs at *his* antics and *those* children willing to volunteer to join him in *his* exploits have great fun. *He* loves to make *them* laugh.

Personal pronouns
Singular: he, him
Plural: they, them

Relative pronouns
who, which

Demonstrative pronouns
those children
that

Possessive pronouns
his
their

Indefinite pronouns
everyone

VERBS AND VERB GROUPS

DEFINITION

A **verb** is an action word that specifically describes what is happening.
A **verb group** is a combination of verbs.

TYPES OF VERBS

- finite
- non-finite

PURPOSE

The purpose of a verb is to describe what is happening in a sentence or clause. Verbs can bring a great deal of information to the sentence and can convey emotion and a level of certainty

CONTEXT

- Every sentence must have a verb.
- Finite verbs have a subject.
- Non-finite verbs cannot work alone. They must have an auxiliary or helping verb which forms a verb group.
- Verbs can be active or passive.
- Verbs give a sense of something happening.

STRUCTURE	HOW VERBS ARE USED
Finite verbs: - must be used in every sentence - must have a subject - have to agree with the subject in person and number.	- The building *crashed* to the ground. *(If there is an answer to the question, 'What crashed?' then the verb is finite.)* - This horse *(singular subject) jumps (singular verb)* the hurdle. - These horses *(plural subject) jump (plural verb)* the hurdles.
Non-finite verbs: There are two kinds of non-finite verbs: **Infinitives** - An infinitive is a verb which has *to* before it. - An infinitive is a verb which follows auxiliary verbs such as *may*, *can*, *shall*, *will*. **Participles** - Every verb has a present and past participle. These can be used with auxiliary verbs to make a compound verb or verb group. - Present participles always end in *-ing*. - Past participles usually end in *-ed*.	**Infinitives** - to *freeze*, to *dance*, to *go*, to *walk* - You may *walk* across the road. **Participles** - I am *singing*. - I have *waited* a long time.

VERBS AND VERB GROUPS

STRUCTURE	HOW VERBS ARE USED
Active and Passive Verbs • *Active* voice is when the subject of the sentence is the doer of the action. • *Passive* voice is when the subject receives the action.	**Active** • Bill *damaged* the car. **Passive** • The car *was damaged* by Bill.
Verbs give a sense of something happening • action verbs • thinking and feeling verbs • saying verbs • being and having verbs *(Relational)* **Modal verbs** • express a degree of probability or a degree of obligation	 • run, jump, drive, promote, erupt • know, wonder, plot, believe • shout, scream, yell, roar, thunder • was, were, has, have • might, must, will, would, shall, should

VERBS – MODALITY

Modal verbs express a degree of probability or a degree of obligation. They are formed by using a modal auxiliary plus the verb. The purpose of modality is to increase the strength or weakness of an argument or an opinion by emphasizing certain points.

Modality can express degrees of:

- *obligation:* ought, should
- *emphasis on something:* simply, absolutely
- *certainty:* will
- *probability of something:* likely, possible, probable
- *importance:* vital, necessary
- *extent:* totally, generally
- *confidence:* sure, believe
- *frequency of something:* always, sometimes, usually

STRUCTURE	HOW MODAL VERBS ARE USED
High Modality shows a high degree of certainty shall/shall not have to/has to must /must not/mustn't ought to	You *must* finish my work today. We *shall* meet again. We *have to* stay remain inside.
Medium modality can/cannot/can't will/will not/won't should/should not/shouldn't need to	You *can* take this. We *should* do this again sometime. You *need to* be quiet.
Low modality shows less certainty could/could not/couldn't would/would not/wouldn't might/might not/mightn't may	I *might* go home now. They *might* visit more often. You *may* want to stay another night.

9780170386166

VERB TENSES

DEFINITION

Verbs tell us about action. *Verb tenses* are tools that we use to express time. They tell us whether an action occurred in the past *(past tense)*, is occurring now *(present tense)* or will occur in the future *(future tense)*.

TYPES OF TENSES

- past – simple
- present – simple, continuous
- future – simple

PURPOSE

The purpose of past, present and future tenses is to add more specific information to text.

STRUCTURE	HOW TENSES ARE USED
Simple past: • describes an action that has already happened • regular form ends in *-ed* • many irregular forms e.g. *came*, *drank*, *brought*.	She *played* hockey. *(simple past)*
Past continuous: • describes an action which was going on at a particular time in the past and had not finished • formed by *was/were* and a *present participle*.	She *was playing* hockey. *(past continuous)*
Simple present: • describes an action that happens and is finished right now; also describes an habitual action • regular form ends in *-s/es* • few irregular forms e.g. *is (to be)*. **Present continuous:** • describes an action that is continuing to happen right now in the present • formed by *is/are* and a *present participle*.	She *plays* hockey. *(simple present)* Sam *is* here. *(simple present)* She *is playing* hockey. *(present continuous)* The ball *is flying* through the air. *(present continuous)* I *have played* hockey for six years. *(present perfect)*
Simple future: • describes an action that will happen in the future • formed by *will* and *a verb* or *going to* and *a verb*. *(expressing intention)* **Future continuous:** • describes an action that will happen and continue in the future • formed by *will be* and a *present participle*.	She *will play* hockey not netball. *(future tense)* He *is going to come* tomorrow. *(future tense)* She *will be playing* hockey even when she is 80 years old! *(future continuous)*

IRREGULAR VERB FORMS

- Simple past tense
  - regular form ends in *-ed*
  - irregular form varies

Example: Verbs and verb tenses

Text type: Narrative

THE HOCKEY GRAND FINALS

Yesterday, the 2007 hockey grand finals *were played* at Downey Park, in Brisbane's inner north. After some very windy preceding days, the day of the grand final turned out to be a beautiful spring day. The first magpie of the season even arrived to start swooping!

All players in the team, Kedron Wavell 11A, *had participated* in the team's win for the 2006 minor premiership. So the familiar grand final feelings *were returning*, ranging from nausea to excitement! Nervous parents on the sideline *watched* in anticipation.

The starting siren *sounded*. The game began. A goal in the first 5 minutes to the opposition!

Injuries! First aid! Run, tackle, run, hit, push, run, and pass. Concentrate! More injuries!

During the half time break the coach *spoke* quietly but firmly. The spectators on the sideline could only guess the contents of his plan.
YOU CAN DO THIS!

The siren *sounded* the start of the second half. Run, tackle, run, hit, push, run, and pass. Concentrate! It worked! The left wing *pounced* on a high ball in the goal circle to score the levelling goal. The supporters on the sideline were in raptures, cheering and clapping wildly!

The result was a joint premiership as the final score was 1-1. Everyone was a winner at this grand final.

Next year I hope we will have improved enough to become premiers.

Compound verbs
were played
had participated

Finite verbs
sounded
spoke

Simple present tense
run
tackle
hit
push
pass

Simple past tense
watched
pounced
sounded

Past continuous tense
were returning

Irregular past tense
wasn't
spoke

ADVERBS

DEFINITION

An **adverb** describes what is happening in the text.

TYPES OF ADVERBS

- adverbs of place
- adverbs of time
- adverbs of manner

- interrogative adverbs
- modal adverbs
- adverbs for opinionative purposes

PURPOSE

The **purpose of an adverb** is to give more information about the circumstances of the action.

CONTEXT

An adverb:
- appears before a verb, adjective or another adverb
- improves the sentence by giving more information
- paints a picture in the reader's imagination
- may be confused with an adjective. If the word describes a noun, then it is an adjective.

If the word describes a verb or another adverb, then it is an adverb.

STRUCTURE	HOW ADVERBS ARE USED
Adverbial ending • Adverbs often end in **–ly**.	soft*ly*, slow*ly*, quick*ly*, immediate*ly*, gradual*ly*, definite*ly*
Adverbs of place • give more meaning about **where** actions happen e.g. *here*, *there*, *outside*, *inside*, *underneath*.	Put the picture *here*, above the fireplace. You need to go to the basketball court *outside*.
Adverbs of time • give more meaning about **when** actions happen e.g. *instantly*, *now*, *later*, *today*.	*Instantly* she turned into a toad. You need to get to the basketball match outside, *now*!
Adverbs of manner • give more meaning about **how** actions happen e.g. *carefully*, *quietly*, *confidently*, *recklessly*, *thoughtfully*, *slowly*.	*Carefully*, he plucked out the feathers. You need to move *quietly* around the house as the baby is asleep.
Interrogative adverbs • enquire about something going on e.g. *how*, *when*, *where*, *why*.	*How* are you? *Why* are you still here when the football match is about to begin?
Modal adverbs • put either agreement, doubt, or disagreement in the reader's mind e.g. *possibly*, *maybe*, *probably*, *perhaps*.	Bin ball is *possibly* on the agenda this afternoon. *Perhaps* you should run, as you are the captain!
Adverbs of opinion • usually placed at the beginning of the sentence and sometimes at the end. • are separated from the rest of the sentence by a comma.	*Clearly*, he doesn't know about the tragedy. *Personally*, I would rather stay here. He donated the money, *generously*.

Example: Adverb   Text type: Persuasive text

POVERTY INTO PEACE

Poverty can *gradually* turn into peace. *Today* one in four children in the world is living in poverty and around 50 000 people die each day because of poverty. Many people existing in this state have to live on two dollars per day.

Currently poverty is becoming more and more of a problem in the world. Many countries choose to spend money on arms rather than saving precious lives. We have to *vigorously* lobby our governments *now* to stop and think what it would be like to try to live on such a pittance. *Soon* it will be too late. We need to put our case forward *immediately* to argue for a fairer distribution of our taxpayer's money so that we can rebuild lives and communities and they can learn to support themselves.

Prime ministers, presidents and other powerful leaders appear to be more interested in acquiring resources like oil and uranium. *Perhaps* their priorities are wrong. *Often* the pursuit of these resources can lead to conflict and then more money has to be spent on defence equipment. *Maybe* we need to focus on providing people with opportunities for employment so that they have money for food and a safe place to sleep.

Finally, we need to ask ourselves *why* we shouldn't try to change the world. Let's turn poverty into peace Personally, I think that it would take only a commitment from each country in the world to work for change.

Adverbs of time
today
currently
now
soon
finally
immediately
often
gradually

Adverbs of manner
vigorously

Adverbs of place
outside
inside
near
far

Interrogative adverbs
why

Modal Adverbs
perhaps
maybe

Opinionative adverb
personally

9780170386166

ADJECTIVES

DEFINITION

An **adjective** provides a description for a noun. It is usually found before a noun or within a noun group

TYPES OF ADJECTIVES

Descriptive, proper, demonstrative, comparative, superlative, possessive, number, definite and indefinite.

PURPOSE

The purpose of an **adjective** is to improve the sentence by giving more information about the subject noun. This paints a picture in the reader's imagination. It can be used after a verb or can combine with a noun to form a noun group.

STRUCTURE	HOW ADJECTIVES ARE USED
Descriptive: • describes the noun and gives a better picture of it.	They have taken a photo of *this beautiful child*. *(noun group)*
Proper: • describes a noun • capitalised because it is created from a name.	The team was chosen for *the Australian Olympics*. *(noun group)*
Demonstrative: • used to point out which noun is being referred to e.g. *this*, *that*, *these*, *those*.	*This* newspaper has *a very interesting report*. *(noun group)*
Comparative: • used when comparing two people or things • usually ends in *-er* or adds the word *more*.	His shoe size is *bigger* than mine. She gets *more beautiful* all the time.
Superlative: • used when comparing more than two people or things • usually ends in *-est* or adds the word *most*.	He has the *biggest* hamburger. Don't choose the *most expensive* ring.
Possessive: • used when referring to a particular person e.g. *my*, *his*, *her*, *its*, *our*, *your*, *their*.	This is *my* newspaper. He has taken *Robert's* hat.
Number: • *one*, *first*, *two*, *second*, etc.	It is the *first* day of Spring.
Definite: • modifies a noun, pronoun or noun phrase e.g. *the*.	Can you buy *the* tickets?

ADJECTIVES

STRUCTURE	HOW ADJECTIVES ARE USED
Indefinite: • modifies a noun, pronoun or noun phrase e.g. *a*, *many*, *few*.	Can you buy me *a* book for my birthday? There are too *many* children to count.
An adjective can be **used after a verb**.	She is *pretty*.
An adjective can be **used when classifying** e.g. classifying flora as native or introduced.	This is a *native* flower.

Example: Adjectives   Text type: Report

THE AUSTRALIAN IMAGE

One of the *most common* images *many* people around the world have of Australians is a person with *fair* hair, *blue* eyes, and *long*, *lean* and *tanned* limbs. Seriously, how many people do you know who actually look like that? Let's see what images emerge after interviewing a group of *twelve-year old* boys about what they think a *typical* Australian person looks like.

Many boys thought the typical Australian was a man wearing *a* hat. *This* hat had corks tied to *a* string coming off the rim. Other *physical* characteristics were the wearing of jeans, as well as a *checked* shirt. Boots completed the picture.

However, after asking the *same* group of boys to indicate if they and **their** families were *typical* Australians, the responses were similar. *All* boys identified themselves and *their* families as **typical** Australians.

It was noted that *not* one boy, nor *one boy's* family member, wore a hat described in the *second* paragraph. Not many wore *checked* shirts, either. The *common* link, however, was the wearing of jeans.

However, is the wearing of jeans distinctly *Australian* or global? How would a *12-year-old boy* living in Canada respond to the *same* question asked about a typical Canadian? When this was researched, *most* boys concurred that jeans were a *typical* clothing item worn by most people. Which then is *more* typical, jeans worn by Australians or jeans worn by Canadians?

To conclude, maybe it is *difficult* to describe the physical appearance of a *typical* Australian or a *typical* Canadian because *both* countries, in fact *many* countries, are populated by people who are beyond stereotyping.

Must go and get *my* cork hat and do the gardening...

Proper adjective
Australian

Describing adjectives
fair, blue, long, lean, tanned, common, typical, physical, checked, same, global *[gives the reader a detailed picture of the person]*

Indefinite adjectives
many
a
all

Definite adjective
the

Demonstrative adjective
this

Number adjectives
one
second
twelve-year-old
both

Superlative adjective
most

Comparative adjective
more

Possessive adjectives
my
their
boy's

Adjective used after a verb
difficult

CONJUNCTIONS

DEFINITION

A **conjunction** is used for joining two parts of a sentence together.

TYPES OF CONJUNCTIONS

- *coordinating* – used to join parts of a sentence
- *correlating* – used to join pairs of ideas in a sentence
- *subordinating* – used to introduce a dependent clause and join it to an independent clause.

PURPOSE

A conjunction is used to join clauses, sentences or phrases. It can join sentences or clauses to make a compound sentence.
Also refer to **Grammar at the text level: Connectives, Paragraphs.**

STRUCTURE	HOW CONJUNCTIONS ARE USED
Coordinating conjunctions: • are used to join parts of sentences. e.g. *and*, *for*, *but*, *or*, *so*, *nor*, *yet*, *with*.	**Joining sentences** My sister and brother love to go to the pool *and* have a swim *with* their friends. He wanted to leave *but* it was too early.
Correlating conjunctions: • are used to join pairs of ideas in a sentence e.g. *either...or* *neither...nor* *not only...but also whether...or* *both...and* *not...but* *as...as.*	**Joining sentence to sentence** *Not only* will he go to visit his friend *but* he will *also* have dinner with the family. **Joining noun to noun** The athletics program is *either* sprints *or* field events. **Joining subject to subject** *Neither* the boys *nor* the girls were able to sing in the competition.
Subordinating conjunctions: • are used to introduce dependent clauses and to join them to independent clauses, showing how these two clauses relate to each other, e.g. *after*, *although*, *before*, *as*, *if*, *how*, *than*, *that*, *until*, *till*, *whether*, *when*, *where*, *while*, *since*.	**Introduces dependent clause and joins it to independent clause** *After* she learned to type, she felt more confident about applying for a new job.

Example: Conjunctions   Text type: Biography

FRED HOLLOWS

Fred Hollows was an ophthalmologist **or** eye specialist, who pioneered eye treatments on a large scale for *both* Indigenous Australians *and* patients in developing countries. It is estimated that he successfully restored the sight of many hundreds of thousands of people *and* in the process became one of Australia's most famous doctors.

Dr Hollows was born in Dunedin New Zealand in 1929 *and* after gaining his B.A. degree, began studying to become a minister of religion. He soon changed to medicine *and after* completing his training he worked in several New Zealand hospitals in the 1950s. *When* he became interested in ophthalmology, he moved to the United Kingdom for specialist training in this area of medicine.

In 1965, Fred Hollows moved to Australia to become Associate Professor of Ophthalmology at the University of New South Wales in Sydney. *As* well *as* holding this position, he later became the Chairman of Division of Ophthalmology of the University of New South Wales, Prince of Wales and Prince Henry teaching hospitals.

In his early years in Australia, he became particularly interested in the very high incidence of trachoma (an eye disease) amongst Indigenous Australians *so* he set up an Aboriginal medical service in Sydney. *Not only* did he help to establish general medical services for indigenous people throughout Australia, he *also* personally performed thousands of eye operations in many Aboriginal communities.

Fred Hollows was awarded the Human Rights Medal *and* named the Australian of the Year in 1990 *but* unfortunately he contracted cancer *and* died in Sydney in 1993. Today he is remembered for his work for poor and underprivileged people not only in Australia *but also* overseas. The Fred Hollows Foundation continues his work. His image has appeared on stamps and there were discussions in 2015 about him featuring on the five-dollar bill.

Co-ordinating conjunctions
and
so
but
or
yet

Subordinating conjunctions
when
after

Correlating conjunctions
not only ... but also
both ... and
as ... as

PREPOSITIONS

DEFINITION

A *preposition* is placed in front of a noun group.

TYPES OF PREPOSITIONS

- time
- place
- direction
- manner

PURPOSE

It is used to indicate where, when and how an action occurs giving more information about the noun group.

STRUCTURE	HOW THEY ARE USED
Prepositions of time: • indicate when something happens e.g. *at*, *after*, *before*, *by*, *for*, *from*, *since*, *until*.	*After* the movie, they went to buy an ice cream. *Before* school, they played cricket.
Prepositions of place and direction: • indicate where something happens e.g. *at*, *on*, *underneath*, *in front of*, *through*, *towards*, *between*, *next to*, *across*, *along*, *among*, *around*, *behind*, *below*, *beside*, *by*, *close to*, *inside outside*, *past*, *round*, *in*, *into*.	He looked *underneath* the desk for his pencil. She stood *in front of* the mirror.
Prepositions of manner: • indicate how something happens e.g. *by*, *like*, *on*, *with*, *in*.	She is coming *by* car. Please write *in* ink not pencil.
Confusing prepositions: Some prepositions can be confusing e.g.: • **among/between:** *between* is used if talking about two people or things; *among* is used with a group • **in/into:** *in* doesn't move; *into* shows movement from one place to the next • **different from** NOT different than • **beside/besides:** *beside* refers to where something is; *besides* means as well as.	The parents came to a decision *between* themselves about their son's future. The teacher told the class to discuss the problem *among* themselves. Put the lizard back *into* the box. The lizard is happy *in* the box; leave it there! The twin was *different from* her sister in looks and personality. There's a car *beside* you, so be careful when you back out. *Besides* a tent, you need food and sleeping gear when you go camping.

Example: Prepositions   **Text type:** Report

THE DROUGHT

Queensland is thirsty. Not Queenslanders but Queensland! Our parched earth is crying out for water. We are *in* the grip of a serious drought.

The many problems *across* the state caused by the drought range *from* crop failures in the country **to** dried up creeks *in* the city. *In* the parks and gardens keeping plants alive *with* little water has become a significant issue. If rain does not come soon, our measures must be more drastic.

Toowoomba, a city of over 119,000 people, has faced a severe water problem this year and one of the proposals to help solve the problem was to recycle water and use it for 25% of their drinking water. There are countries *around* the world using this system but at a much lower percentage. Singapore for example uses 5% of recycled water for drinking. The suggestion for Toowoomba was well *above* that figure.

In the spirit of democracy, the city council decided to hold a referendum to ask people their opinions. *Despite* the big media campaign, the vote failed to carry. After the vote was defeated, many people thought that it would have been much better to reduce the percentage of water *in* the beginning and then increase it as people became more used to the idea.

Since that time, many Brisbane residents have begun to wonder if the council will put the same suggestions forward. What do you think? Should Brisbane say 'yes' to recycled water flowing through their taps? Before that happens, the voters would need to be more informed about the issue.

Place/direction prepositions
to
from
in
above
into
across
around

Time prepositions
after
since
in

Manner prepositions
in
with

Complex prepositions
despite

INDEX